ST. JEROME SCHOOL

GRADE 7
LESSON PLAN

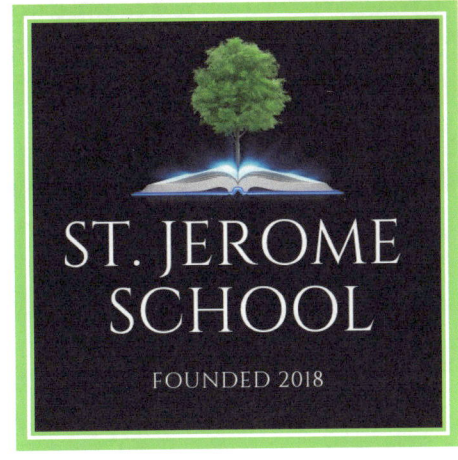

St. Jerome Library

WWW.STJEROMELIBRARY.ORG

COPYRIGHT ©2019AD-2024AD BY ST. JEROME LIBRARY PRESS

FAIRBANKS, INDIANA

ALL RIGHTS RESERVED.

No part of this book may be reproduced or transmitted in any form or by any means, electronic or mechanical, including photocopying, recording, or by any information storage or retrieval system, without written permission from the publisher.

Thank you!

A Word about St. Jerome School

St. Jerome School is a branch of St. Jerome Library, the parent nonprofit organization to our mission of helping Catholic families to homeschool by providing affordable options in the most important vocation of raising saints for heaven. St. Jerome School & Library is a publisher, a true library, a bookstore, and a school, in the sense of providing teaching materials and lesson plans.

We use a simple, classic approach to education. Many of the items included in our lesson plans are from time-tested traditional sources. Some books, like our readers have been used in Catholic Schools since the early 1900s. Others are recent publications published with very sound, traditional Catholic doctrine and modest illustrations, all with no infections of modernism or other heresies. We are excited to share these wonderful books with you and your students. We truly hope that you will enjoy teaching with us!

Our school year is based on 36 weeks.

These items are for sale in our store, which you can find at www.stjeromelibrary.org

Books Highly Recommended for Family Daily/Weekly Use with our Curriculum

We highly recommend Catholic families say each day their morning prayers, evening prayers, Angelus (or Regina Caeli during Eastertide), and Family Rosary. Making Spiritual Communions is greatly encouraged during these difficult times of ours, and you can make frequent visits to the cemetery to pray for the Holy Souls in Purgatory.

In aiding the family with young children, we highly recommend these incredible books to boost the spiritual life:

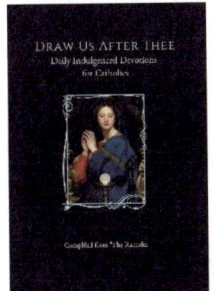

Draw Us after Thee: Daily Indulgenced Devotions for Catholics which has a different daily prayer and picture for every day of the year to enchance morning prayers. Catholics reap the benefits of never being in danger of a stale prayer life while learning about the different feasts of the Church and incredible indulgences She offers to us. Indulgences can be given to the Holy Souls in Purgatory as well!

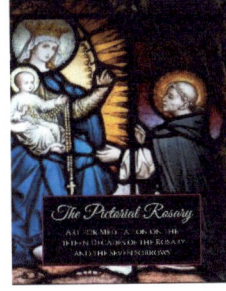

Pictorial Lives of the Saints, which has wonderful short stories & reflections of the saints' lives for daily meditation. Great for inspiring questions and "teaching moments". Stories are fairly short as to keep children's attention.

The Pictorial Rosary is a great aid for meditation during the Family Rosary, as well as including the excellent prayers to Our Lady of Sorrows which adds an excellent addition to family night prayers.

Feeding God's People

Providence Pastures Co. is a nonprofit formed by us, exclusively for advancing the Kingship of Christ and helping Our Lady and St. Joseph harbor and advance the family and domestic Church. We have come to see ourselves as stewards of creation and hope to share the undeniable goodness and health benefits of pasture-raised, nutrient-dense food. In these trying times, we see our work as an apostolate from Our Blessed Mother to feed Her children by providing affordable, healthy foods, such as organic grass-fed and finished, pasture-raised beef, chicken, pork, maple syrup, wheat products, produce, and more. Visit our certified organic farm's website at www.pasturesofprovidence.com Contact us through the website if you are interested in food being shipped to you. May God be with you!

Grade Seven

Grammar – This year continues the use of the old Catholic *Voyages in English* series from the 1950s with our updated and beautiful *St. Jerome Grammar* series. The *St. Jerome Grammar 7* text will give your child the foundation necessary for excellent grammar skills. *St. Jerome Grammar 7 Teacher's Text Manual* will give the teacher instructions for teaching from the text book, as well as the answers to the exercises within the text. The *St. Jerome Grammar 7 Workbook* is filled with fun and edifying color pictures to drive home what your student has learned from the text. The *St. Jerome Grammar 7 Workbook Answer Key* will help immensely in speeding the process of grading with handy side-by-side answers to match the workbooks. A grammar notebook can be used for assigning writing assignments as needed.

Music – This grade continues the fun and secular series of *Doctor Mozart's Music Theory*. *Doctor Mozart Music Theory Workbook 1B* continues to give your child a strong musical foundation. By the end of the three books that are used throughout middle school, your student will have learned much which will serve them in the future. Also, we would highly recommend you introduce the student to some classical forms of music, such as Gregorian Chant, Masses, traditional Catholic songs, etc. Perhaps buy your student a new inexpensive instrument and see if they can try to learn to play it. Have fun!

History – *Bible History* will also be used to briefly go over our history, but not in a very intense way, simply for reading enjoyment and historical knowledge. This is a wonderful, classic way to get your child more familiar with the Bible before more intensive study in future years. Children will also be reading the combo comic book *Man of Peace/The Truth Behind the Trial of Cardinal Nindszenty* which awakens them to the dangers of Communism, as well as the short but sweet *Mary's Greatest Apostle: St. Louis Grignion de Montfort*.

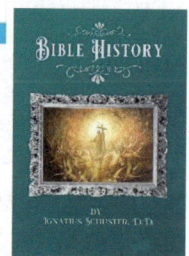

Reading – *St. Jerome School Reader 7* text is an incredible, classic Catholic reader that has been used for over a hundred years with students! The historical content helps children learn about times long past, including the beautiful speech that was used. We have found that often it helps if you alternate between reading lessons with your student, and then having him or her read the next one on their own. This gives good oral reading practice. Other literature books include *Flame of White, The Gauntlet,* and *St. John Bosco Stories*. These are all incredible works, difficult to put down, which also teach about history (including St. Pope Pius X and St. John Bosco). We recommend assigning book reports (located in the back for copying) after reading the books. A discussion of the books between teacher and student should also be present.

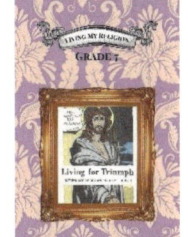

Religion - *Living My Religion Grade 7* is from the 1940s' imprimatured *Living My Religion* series which teaches catechism in a fun and traditional way. The text is written in an easy-to-read format so that the child feels invited and excited to practice reading with the simple text. *The World is His Parish: The Story of Pope Pius XII* is also included. It is a graphic novel relating the life of Pope Pius XII. It is simply wonderful for children to become more familiar with this pope of recent times and the crosses he carried. Children also get to read the wonderful *Saint Stories for the Young, Vol. 1.* May he rest in peace.

Math – This year's text will be *Saxon Math 8/7*. We highly recommend you also purchase *Saxon Math 8/7 Solutions Manual* to help with fast grading. If you trust your student, it may prove beneficial to have them grade their own math after they have done it to learn what they have done wrong. Teachers, of course, grade tests so they can gauge what the student has been learning well. This works well especially in large, busy families where a mother is trying to grade many children's lessons each day. It can be overwhelming! *Saxon Math 87 Tests & Worksheets* should also be purchased as the tests are in it, as well as the activities and math drills. We will only be doing one of each math drill. Teachers may assign more if she sees there is a great need for the student to work more on a particular skill.

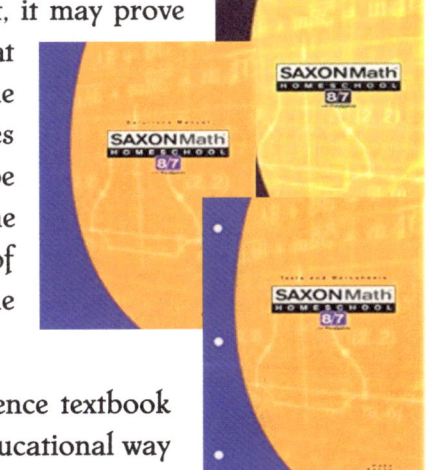

Science – *Science in God's World 7* is a classic and colorful science textbook which reflects the Catholic faith. It presents science in a simple, educational way with questions and basic facts, as well as providing opportunities to discuss the subjects with the teacher and offering optional experiments. We hope you will enjoy this series as we at St. Jerome Library Press have updated many of the pictures to include modern-day photos so that students will have excellent, solid scientific education along with the beautiful Catholic Faith infused throughout. The *Science in God's World 7 Workbook* will offer a splendid review of the concepts learned throughout the book, including a little fun humor to make learning a bit more fun. The *Science in God's World 7 Answer Key* is necessary for grading everything in this science course.

Spelling – This year's spelling continues with *Spelling Forest Grade 7*. This speller is filled with beautiful forest-themed pages, including many Catholic exercises, which make learning vocabulary, spelling, and a bit of handwriting practice one of our students' favorite activities. The words include Catholic terminology, along with words compiled from grade-appropriate standards used in national spelling bees and the like. If the teacher does not already own it, *St. Jerome Catholic Spellers Answer Key* will be essential for grading the "Fill in the Blank" and "Synonyms & Antonyms" sections of the workbook. A Spelling Notebook will be used to write the words for tests or as practice for those words that were done incorrectly on the pretest.

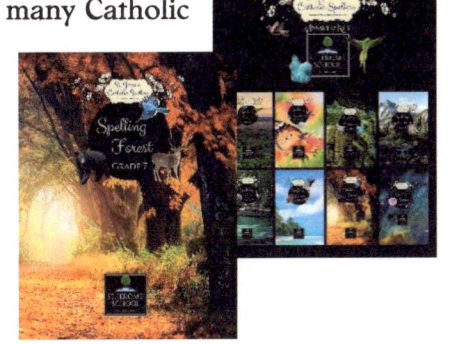

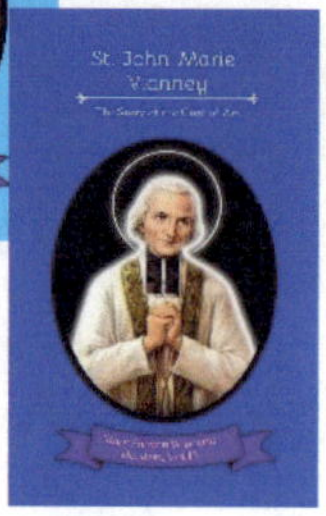

Summer Reading – For the summer, we would like to students to keep up their reading habits somewhat. The Summer Reading List for Grade 7 are the Windeatt books: *The Little Flower, The Cure of Ars, Saint Hyacinth of Poland,* and *Saint Louis de Montfort.* The book report form is in the back of this book.

Student will also need:

Compass (drawing circles)

Folder for Completed Papers

Graph Paper

Pencils

Pens

Protractor

Ruler w/cm & in

Scientific Calculator

Scissors

Notebooks for Grammar, Math, Science, and Spelling

In the lesson plan, * means refer to Comments section for the week

The Report Card is in the back for easy record keeping.

Sample

Spaces below the assignments are for grades, comments, time spent, etc.

Kindergarten Lesson Plans			
Subject	Monday	Tuesday	Wednesday
Hand-writing & Phonics	-HK: Sing the ABC Song with student while on p. ix & count #'s, then p. xi-xiv	-HK: ABC Song with p. x, then p. 1-3 -ABC: Read p. 2-9	-HK: Review ABC's with student daily until understood, then p. 4-6 -ABC: Review p. 4-9
	N/A	*95%*	*30min, 98%*
Hand-writing & Phonics	-HK: p. 13-15 -ABC: p. 11-17	-HK: p. 16-18 -ABC: Review p. 11-17	-HK: p. 19-21 -ABC: Review p. 11-17
	100%, hard worker!	*87%, rushed and distracted*	*92%*

Book Abbreviations for Grade 7 Lesson Plans

Bible History = BH

Doctor Mozart 1B Music Theory = DM1B

Flame of White = FW

The Gauntlet = G

Living My Religion Grade 7 = LMR7

Man of Peace/The Truth Behind the Trial of Cardinal Mindszenty = MP/TCM

Mary's Greatest Apostle: St. Louis Grignion de Montfort = MGA

Saint Stories for the Young, Vol. 1 = SSY1

Saxon Math 8/7 Tests & Worksheets = SMTW7

Saxon Math 8/7 Text = SM7

Science in God's World 7 = SGW7

Science in God's World 7 Workbook = SGW7WB

Spelling Forest Grade 7 = SF

St. Jerome Grammar 7 Text = SJG7

St. Jerome Grammar 7 Workbook = SJG7WB

St. Jerome School Reader 7 = SJSR7

St. John Bosco Stories = SJBS

The World is His Parish = WHP

Week 1

Subject	Monday	Tuesday	Wednesday
Religion			-LMR7: p. 1-8 (Teacher & student may alternatingly read to each other. Teacher orally asks test questions at the end of chapters.)
Spelling	-SF: p. 3-6, Student reads words aloud to teacher for correct*	-SF: p. 7-8	
Grammar	-SJG7: p. 213-222 Stop at "4. Case" (Reading can be done any time during the week.) It is recommended that teacher reads*	-SJG7WB: p. 5	-SJG7WB: p. 6
Reading	-SJSR7: p. 11-21 (Each day, one lesson to be orally read by teacher to student, and another by student to teacher.)*	-SJSR7: p. 20-27	
History		-BH: p. 1-8, Student will read and stop at the end of a chapter, but does not need to answer questions, just understand the information.	
Math	-SM7: L. 1, student reads lessons to himself, then does Lesson Practice, and evens (or odds) only Mixed Practice in MN	-SM7: L. 2 -SMTW7: Facts Practice Test A (these may be done more than once if teacher wishes)	-SM7: L. 3
Science			
Music Theory			-DM1B: p. 2-3

Week 1

Subject	Thursday	Friday	Comments
Religion		-WHP: Read p. 1-9	
Spelling	-SF: Administer pre-test. Student writes words in Spelling notebook 3x each that are wrong.	-SF: Take Post-test for grade.	*pronunciation, then writes words as neatly as possible
Grammar	-SJG7WB: p. 7	-SJG7WB: p. 8	*to student & does some of the exercises in the book to gauge understanding. Workbooks assignments are done on their own.
Reading			*This gives the student both the good example of storytelling and the chance to practice it himself.
History			
Math	-SM7: L. 4	-SM7: L. 5	
Science	-SGW7: Read p. 5-20	-SGW7WB: p. 3 -Questions throughout the textbook may be done as an optional review.	
Music Theory			

Week 2

Subject	Monday	Tuesday	Wednesday
Religion			-LMR7: p. 8-18
Spelling	-SF: p. 9-12, Lesson 2	-SF: p. 13-14	
Grammar	-SJG7: p. 1-27, 222-224 (Stop at "Nominative in Apposition")*	-SJG7WB: p. 9	-SJG7WB: p. 10
Reading	-SJSR7: p. 28-36	-SJSR7: p. 37-46	
History		-BH: p. 8-13	
Math	-SM7: L. 6	-SM7: L. 7	-SM7: L. 8 -SMTW7: FPT B
Science			
Music Theory			-DM1B: p. 4

Week 2

Subject	Thursday	Friday	Comments
Religion		-WHP: Read p. 10-18	
Spelling	-SF: Administer pre-test. Student writes words in Spelling notebook 3x each that are wrong.	-SF: Take Post-test for grade.	
Grammar	-SJG7WB: p. 11	-SJG7WB: p. 12	*Teacher will assign writing assignments from SJG7 according to the student's needs, to be written in his Grammar notebook.
Reading			
History			
Math	-SM7: L. 9	-SM7: L. 10	
Science	-SGW7: Read p. 20-27	-SGW7WB: p. 4	
Music Theory			

Week 3

Subject	Monday	Tuesday	Wednesday
Religion			-LMR7: p. 19-23
Spelling	-SF: p. 15-18, Lesson 3	-SF: p. 19-20	
Grammar	-SJG7: p. 28-55 (fix immodest pictures throughout the book), p. 224-230 (Stop at "Objective Case")	-SJG7WB: p. 13 (p. 14 for extra credit, if desired)	-SJG7WB: p. 15
Reading	-SJSR7: p. 47-53	-SJSR7: p. 54-63	
History		-BH: p. 13-17	
Math	-SMTW7: Test 1 (Show all work on loose leaf paper or notebook)	-SM7: Investigation 1* -SMTW7: Activity Sheets 1-6	-SM7: L. 11 -SMTW7: FPT C
Science			
Music Theory			-DM1B: p. 5

Week 3

Subject	Thursday	Friday	Comments
Religion		-WHP: Read p. 19-27	
Spelling	-SF: Administer pre-test. Student writes words in Spelling notebook 3x each that are wrong.	-SF: Take Post-test for grade.	
Grammar	-SJG7WB: p. 16	-SJG7WB: p. 17	
Reading			
History			
Math	-SM7: L. 12	-SM7: L. 13	*Sometimes investigations can be complicated and confusing. They can be counted as extra credit only if the teacher wishes.
Science	-SGW7: Read p. 27-35, Do experiments as time allows at teacher's discretion throughout the year	-SGW7WB: p. 5	
Music Theory			

Week 4

Subject	Monday	Tuesday	Wednesday
Religion			-LMR7: p. 23-30
Spelling	-SF: p. 21-24, Lesson 4	-SF: p. 25-26	
Grammar	-SJG7: p. 56-85, 230-233	-SJG7WB: p. 18	-SJG7WB: p. 19
Reading	-SJSR7: p. 64-70	-SJSR7: p. 71-81	
History		-BH: p. 18-25	
Math	-SM7: L. 14	-SM7: L. 15	-SMTW7: Test 2
Science			
Music Theory			-DM1B: p. 6

			Week 4	
Subject	Thursday		Friday	Comments
Religion			-WHP: Read p. 28-35 (end!)	
Spelling	-SF: Administer pre-test. Student writes words in Spelling notebook 3x each that are wrong.		-SF: Take Post-test for grade.	
Grammar	-SJG7WB: p. 20		-SJG7WB: p. 21	
Reading				
History				
Math	-SM7: L. 16		-SM7: L. 17	
Science	-SGW7: Read p. 36-47		-SGW7WB: p. 6	
Music Theory				

Week 5

Subject	Monday	Tuesday	Wednesday
Religion			-LMR7: p. 30-36
Spelling	-SF: p. 27-30, L. 5	-SF: p. 31-32	
Grammar	-SJG7: p. 86-117, 234-238	-SJG7WB: p. 22	-SJG7WB: p. 23
Reading	-SJSR7: p. 82-89	-SJSR7: p. 90-98	
History		-BH: p. 25-29	
Math	-SM7: L. 18	-SM7: L. 19	-SM7: L. 20 -SMTW7: FPT D
Science			
Music Theory			-DM1B: p. 7

Week 5

Subject	Thursday	Friday	Comments
Religion			
Spelling	-SF: Administer pre-test. Student writes words in Spelling notebook 3x each that are wrong.	-SF: Take Post-test for grade.	
Grammar	-SJG7WB: p. 24 (p. 25 for extra credit)	-SJG7WB: p. 26 (p. 27 extra credit)	
Reading			
History		-BH: p. 30-34	
Math	-SMTW7: Test 3	-SM7: Investigation 2	
Science	-SGW7: Read p. 51-58	-SGW7WB: p. 7	
Music Theory			

Week 6

Subject	Monday	Tuesday	Wednesday
Religion			-LMR7: p. 37-43
Spelling	-SF: p. 33-36, L. 6	-SF: p. 37-38	
Grammar	-SJG7: p. 239-249	-SJG7WB: p. 28	-SJG7WB: p. 29
Reading	-SJSR7: p. 99-106	-SJSR7: p. 107-113	
History		-BH: p. 35-40	
Math	-SM7: L. 21	-SM7: L. 22	-SM7: L. 23 -SMTW7: FPT E
Science			
Music Theory			-DMIB: p. 8

Week 6

Subject	Thursday	Friday	Comments
Religion			
Spelling	-SF: Administer pre-test. Student writes words in Spelling notebook 3x each that are wrong.	-SF: Take Post-test for grade.	
Grammar	-SJG7WB: p. 30	-SJG7WB: p. 31	
Reading			
History		-BH: p. 40-46	
Math	-SM7: L. 24	-SM7: L. 25	
Science	-SGW7: Read p. 58-70	-SGW7WB: p. 8	
Music Theory			

Week 7

Subject	Monday	Tuesday	Wednesday
Religion			-LMR7: p. 43-50
Spelling	-SF: p. 39-42, L. 7	-SF: p. 43-44	
Grammar	-SJG7: p. 118-151, 250-255 (Stop at "Predicate Nominative")	-SJG7WB: p. 32	-SJG7WB: p. 33
Reading	-SJSR7: p. 114-122	-SJSR7: p. 123-129	
History		-BH: p. 47-52	
Math	-SMTW7: Test 4	-SM7: L. 26	-SM7: L. 27 -SMTW7: FPT F
Science			
Music Theory			-DMIB: p. 9

Week 7

Subject	Thursday	Friday	Comments
Religion			
Spelling	-SF: Administer pre-test. Student writes words in Spelling notebook 3x each that are wrong.	-SF: Take Post-test for grade.	
Grammar	-SJG7WB: p. 34	-SJG7WB: p. 35	
Reading			
History		-BH: p. 53-58	
Math	-SM7: L. 28	-SM7: L. 29	
Science	-SGW7: Read p. 70-80	-SGW7WB: p. 9	
Music Theory			

Week 8

Subject	Monday	Tuesday	Wednesday
Religion			-LMR7: p. 50-54
Spelling	-SF: p. 45-48, L. 8	-SF: p. 49-50	
Grammar	-SJG7: p. 152-169, 255-259 (Stop at "Object of a Preposition")	-SJG7WB: p. 36	-SJG7WB: p. 37
Reading	-SJSR7: p. 130-136	-SJSR7: p. 137-144	
History		-BH: p. 58-64	
Math	-SM7: L. 30	-SMTW7: Test 5	-SM7: Investigation 3
Science			
Music Theory			-DM1B: p. 10

Week 8

Subject	Thursday	Friday	Comments
Religion			
Spelling	-SF: Administer pre-test. Student writes words in Spelling notebook 3x each that are wrong.	-SF: Take Post-test for grade.	
Grammar	-SJG7WB: p. 38	-SJG7WB: p. 39	
Reading			
History		-BH: p. 65-70	
Math	-SM7: L. 31	-SM7: L. 32	
Science	-SGW7: Read p. 80-92	-SGW7WB: p. 10	
Music Theory			

Week 9

Subject	Monday	Tuesday	Wednesday
Religion			-LMR7: p. 55-64
Spelling			
Grammar	-SJG7: p. 170-189 (explain modern changes), 259-264 (Stop at "5. Drill on Relative Pronouns")	-SJG7WB: p. 40 (p. 41 for extra credit)	-SJG7WB: p. 42
Reading	-SJSR7: p. 145-154	-SJSR7: p. 155-161	
History		-BH: p. 71-77	
Math	-SM7: L. 33	-Review any needed math lessons	-SM7: L. 34 -SMTW7: FPT G
Science			
Music Theory			-DM1B: p. 11

Week 9

Subject	Thursday	Friday	Comments
Religion			
Spelling			
Grammar	-SJG7WB: p. 43-44	-SJG7WB: p. 45	
Reading			
History		-BH: p. 78-83	
Math	-SM7: L. 35	-SMTW7: Test 6	
Science	-SGW7: Study for First Quarter Exam	-First Quarter Exam	
Music Theory			

Week 10

Subject	Monday	Tuesday	Wednesday
Religion			-LMR7: p. 65-72
Spelling	-SF: p. 51-54, L. 9	-SF: p. 55-56	
Grammar	-SJG7: p. 190-210 (explain modern changes), 264-265 (Stop at "6. Agreement with Distributive and Indefinite Pronouns")	-SJG7WB: p. 46	-SJG7WB: p. 47
Reading	-SJSR7: p. 162-172	-SJSR7: p. 173-183	
History		-BH: p. 83-90	
Math	-SM7: L. 36	-SM7: L. 37	-SM7: L. 38
Science			
Music Theory			-DM1B: p. 12

Week 10

Subject	Thursday	Friday	Comments
Religion	-SSY1: Read p. 3-10		
Spelling	-SF: Administer pre-test. Student writes words in Spelling notebook 3x each that are wrong.	-SF: Take Post-test for grade.	
Grammar	-SJG7WB: p. 48	-SJG7WB: p. 49	
Reading			
History		-BH: p. 90-95	
Math	-SM7: L. 39	-SM7: L. 40	
Science	-SGW7: Read p. 92-99	-SGW7WB: p. 11	
Music Theory			

Subject	Monday	Tuesday	Wednesday
Religion			-LMR7: p. 73-79
Spelling	-SF: p. 57-60, L. 10	-SF: p. 61-62	
Grammar	-SJG7: p. 265-268	-SJG7WB: p. 50-51 (Student may skip answering syntax question on line if teacher is okay with that, p. 52 extra credit)	-SJG7WB: p. 53
Reading	-SJSR7: p. 184-189	-SJSR7: p. 190-195	
History		-BH: p. 95-102	
Math	-SMTW7: Test 7	-SM7: Investigation 4	-SM7: L. 41 -SMTW7: FPT H
Science			
Music Theory			-DM1B: p. 13

Week 11

Week 11

Subject	Thursday	Friday	Comments
Religion	-SSY1: Read p. 11-16		
Spelling	-SF: Administer pre-test. Student writes words in Spelling notebook 3x each that are wrong.	-SF: Take Post-test for grade.	
Grammar	-SJG7WB: p. 54	-SJG7WB: p. 55 (p. 56 extra credit)	
Reading			
History		-BH: p. 103-109	
Math	-SM7: L. 42	-SM7: L. 43 -SMTW7: FPT 1	
Science	-SGW7: Read p. 99-104	-SGW7WB: p. 12	
Music Theory			

Week 12

Subject	Monday	Tuesday	Wednesday
Religion			-LMR7: p. 79-90
Spelling	-SF: p. 63-66, L. 11	-SF: p. 67-68	
Grammar	-SJG7: p. 269-276 (Stop at "Comparison of Adjectives")	-SJG7WB: p. 57	-SJG7WB: p. 58
Reading	-SJSR7: p. 196-204	-SJSR7: p. 205-213	
History		-BH: p. 109-116	
Math	-SM7: L. 44	-SM7: L. 45	-SMTW7: Test 8
Science			
Music Theory			-DM1B: p. 14

Week 12

Subject	Thursday	Friday	Comments
Religion	-SSY1: Read p. 17-22		
Spelling	-SF: Administer pre-test. Student writes words in Spelling notebook 3x each that are wrong.	-SF: Take Post-test for grade.	
Grammar	-SJG7WB: p. 59	-SJG7WB: p. 60	
Reading			
History		-BH: p. 116-123	
Math	-SM7: L. 46	-SM7: L. 47	
Science	-SGW7: Read p. 109-119	-SGW7WB: p. 13	
Music Theory			

Week 13

Subject	Monday	Tuesday	Wednesday
Religion			-LMR7: p. 91-98
Spelling	-SF: p. 69-72, L. 12	-SF: p. 73-74	
Grammar	-SJG7: p. 276-283 (Stop at "5. Words Used as Nouns and Adjectives)	-SJG7WB: p. 61	-SJG7WB: p. 62
Reading	-SJSR7: p. 215-220	-SJSR7: p. 221-225	
History		-BH: p. 123-128	
Math	-SM7: L. 48	-SM7: L. 49	-SM7: L. 50
Science			
Music Theory			-DM1B: p. 15

Week 13

Subject	Thursday	Friday	Comments
Religion	-SSY1: Read p. 23-28		
Spelling	-SF: Administer pre-test. Student writes words in Spelling notebook 3x each that are wrong.	-SF: Take Post-test for grade.	
Grammar	-SJG7WB: p. 63	-SJG7WB: p. 64	
Reading			
History		-BH: p. 129-135	
Math	-SMTW7: Test 9	-SM7: Investigation 5	
Science	-SGW7: Read p. 119-126	-SGW7WB: p. 14	
Music Theory			

Week 14

Subject	Monday	Tuesday	Wednesday
Religion			-LMR7: p. 98-108
Spelling	-SF: p. 75-78, L. 13	-SF: p. 79-80	
Grammar	-SJG7: p. 283-292 (Stop at "Copulative Verbs")	-SJG7WB: p. 65 (p. 66 extra credit)	-SJG7WB: p. 67
Reading	-SJSR7: p. 226-233	-SJSR7: p. 234-240 (end!)	
History		-BH: p. 136-141	
Math	-SM7: L. 51 -SMTW7: FPT J	-SM7: L. 52	-SM7: L. 53 -SMTW7: FPT K
Science			
Music Theory			-DMIB: p. 16

Week 14

Subject	Thursday	Friday	Comments
Religion	-SSY1: Read p. 29-34		
Spelling	-SF: Administer pre-test. Student writes words in Spelling notebook 3x each that are wrong.	-SF: Take Post-test for grade.	
Grammar	-SJG7WB: p. 68	-SJG7WB: p. 69	
Reading	-G: p. 11-23		
History		-BH: p. 141-147	
Math	-SM7: L. 54	-SM7: L. 55	
Science	-SGW7: Read p. 126-142	-SGW7WB: p. 15	
Music Theory			

Week 15

Subject	Monday	Tuesday	Wednesday
Religion			-LMR7: p. 109-114
Spelling	-SF: p. 81-84, L. 14	-SF: p. 85-86	
Grammar	-SJG7: p. 292-295 (Stop at "Attributes or Qualities of a Verb")	-SJG7WB: p. 70	-SJG7WB: p. 71
Reading	-G: p. 24-35	-G: p. 36-42	
History		-BH: p. 147-153	
Math	-SMTW7: Test 10	-SM7: L. 56	-SM7: L. 57
Science			
Music Theory			-DMIB: p. 17

Week 15

Subject	Thursday	Friday	Comments
Religion	-SSY1: Read p. 35-40		
Spelling	-SF: Administer pre-test. Student writes words in Spelling notebook 3x each that are wrong.	-SF: Take Post-test for grade.	
Grammar	-SJG7WB: p. 72	-SJG7WB: p. 73	
Reading	-G: p. 43-51		
History		-BH: p. 153-158	
Math	-SM7: L. 58	-SM7: L. 59 -SMTW7: FPT L	
Science	-SGW7: Read p. 143-158	-SGW7WB: p. 16	
Music Theory			

Subject	Monday	Tuesday	Wednesday
Religion			-LMR7: p. 114-121
Spelling	-SF: p. 87-90, L. 15	-SF: p. 91-92	
Grammar	-SJG7: p. 295-299	-SJG7WB: p. 74	-SJG7WB: p. 75
Reading	-G: p. 52-64	-G: p. 65-81	
History		-BH: p. 159-165	
Math	-SM7: L. 60	-SMTW7: Test 11	-SM7: Investigation 6
Science			
Music Theory			-DM1B: p. 18

Week 16

Subject	Thursday	Friday	Comments
Religion	-SSY1: Read p. 41-47		
Spelling	-SF: Administer pre-test. Student writes words in Spelling notebook 3x each that are wrong.	-SF: Take Post-test for grade.	
Grammar	-SJG7WB: p. 76	-SJG7WB: p. 77	
Reading	-G: p. 82-91		
History		-BH: p. 165-172	
Math	-SM7: L. 61	-SM7: L. 62	
Science	-SGW7: Read p. 158-163	-SGW7WB: p. 17	
Music Theory			

Week 17

Subject	Monday	Tuesday	Wednesday
Religion			-LMR7: p. 122-126
Spelling	-SF: p. 93-96, L. 16	-SF: p. 97-98	
Grammar	-SJG7: 300-313 (Stop at "Phrases and Parenthetical Expressions")	-SJG7WB: p. 78 (p. 79 extra credit)	-SJG7WB: p. 80
Reading	-G: p. 92-105	-G: p. 106-122	
History		-BH: p. 172-179	
Math	-SM7: L. 63	-SM7: L. 64	-SM7: L. 65
Science			
Music Theory			-DM1B: p. 19

Week 17

Subject	Thursday	Friday	Comments
Religion	-SSY1: Read p. 48-53		
Spelling	-SF: Administer pre-test. Student writes words in Spelling notebook 3x each that are wrong.	-SF: Take Post-test for grade.	
Grammar	-SJG7WB: p. 81	-SJG7WB: p. 82	
Reading	-G: p. 123-134		
History		-BH: p. 180-185	
Math	-SMTW7: Test 12	-SM7: L. 66 -SMTW7: FPT M	
Science	-SGW7: Read p. 163-173	-SGW7WB: p. 18	
Music Theory			

Week 18

Subject	Monday	Tuesday	Wednesday
Religion			
Spelling			
Grammar	-SJG7: 313-315 (Stop at "Compound Subjects Connected by 'Each' and 'Every'")	-SJG7WB: p. 83	-SJG7WB: p. 84
Reading	-G: p. 135-149	-G: p. 150-161	
History		-BH: p. 186-191	
Math	-SM7: L. 67	-SM7: L. 68	-SM7: L. 69
Science			
Music Theory			-DM1B: p. 20

Week 18

Subject	Thursday	Friday	Comments
Religion	-SSY1: Read p. 54-60		
Logic & Spelling			
Grammar	-SJG7WB: p. 85		
Reading	-G: p. 162-175		
History		-BH: p. 192-199	
Math			
Science	Study for Second Quarter Exam (p. 92-173)	-Second Quarter Exam	
Music Theory			

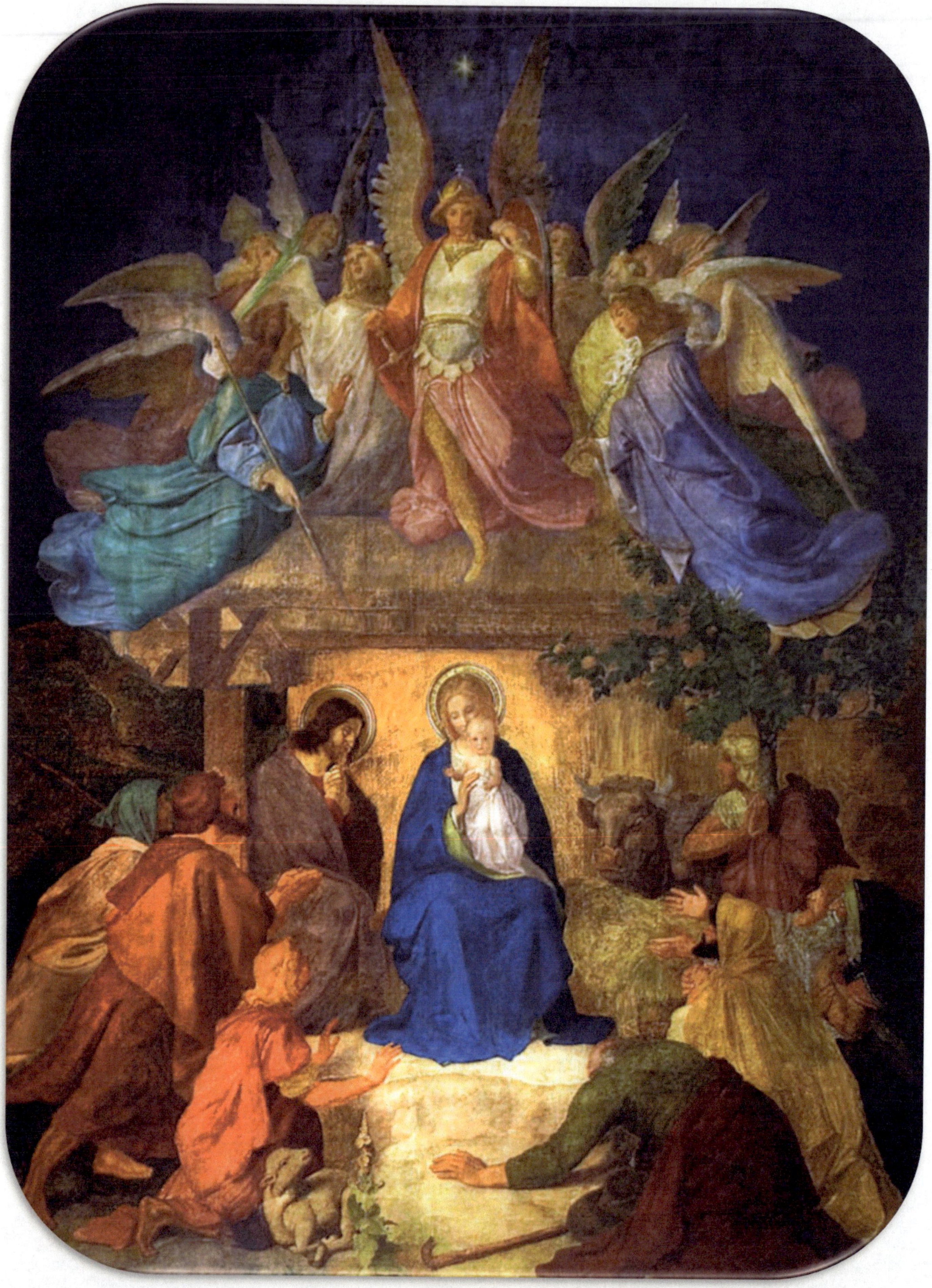

Grade 7 Third Quarter

Subject	Monday	Tuesday	Wednesday
Religion			-LMR7: p. 127-134
Spelling	-SF: p. 99-102, L. 17	-SF: p. 103-104	
Grammar	-SJG7: p. 315-318 (Stop at "Distributive and Indefinite Pronouns")	-SJG7WB: p. 86	-SJG7WB: p. 87
Reading	-G: p. 176-189	-G: p. 190-204	
History		-BH: p. 199-206	
Math	-SM7: L. 70	-SMTW7: Test 13	-SM7: Investigation 7
Science			
Music Theory			-DM1B: p. 21

Week 19

	Week 19		
Subject	Thursday	Friday	Comments
Religion	-SSY1: Read p. 61-64		
Spelling	-SF: Administer pre-test. Student writes words in Spelling notebook 3x each that are wrong.	-SF: Take Post-test for grade.	
Grammar	-SJG7WB: p. 88	-SJG7WB: p. 89	
Reading	-G: p. 205-221		
History		-BH: p. 206-212	
Math	-SM7: L. 71	-SM7: L. 72 -SMTW7: FPT N	
Science	-SGW7: Read p. 179-188	-SGW7WB: p. 19	
Music Theory			

Week 20

Subject	Monday	Tuesday	Wednesday
Religion			-LMR7: p. 134-139
Spelling	-SF: p. 105-108, L. 18	-SF: p. 109-110	
Grammar	-SJG7: p. 318-322 (Stop at "2. Uses of Should & Would")	-SJG7WB: p. 90	-SJG7WB: p. 91
Reading	-G: p. 222-234	-G: p. 235-248 (end!) Book report	
History		-BH: p. 213-218	
Math	-SM7: L. 73 -SMTW7: FPT O	-SM7: L. 74	-SM7: L. 75
Science			
Music Theory			-DM1B: p. 22

Week 20

Subject	Thursday	Friday	Comments
Religion	-SSY1: Read p. 65-70		
Spelling	-SF: Administer pre-test. Student writes words in Spelling notebook 3x each that are wrong.	-SF: Take Post-test for grade.	
Grammar	-SJG7WB: p. 92	-SJG7WB: p. 93	
Reading	-FW: p. 1-6		
History		-BH: p. 219-225	
Math	-SMTW7: Test 14	-SM7: L. 76	
Science	-SGW7: Read p. 188-196	-SGW7WB: p. 20	
Music Theory			

Subject	Monday	Tuesday	Wednesday
Religion			-LMR7: p. 140-144
Spelling	-SF: p. 111-114, L. 19	-SF: p. 115-116	
Grammar	-SJG7: p. 323-331	-SJG7WB: p. 94	-SJG7WB: p. 95
Reading	-FW: p. 7-12	-FW: p. 13-18	
History		-BH: p. 225-231	
Math	-SM7: L. 77	-SM7: L. 78	-SM7: L. 79 -SMTW7: FPT P
Science			
Music Theory			-DM1B: p. 23

Week 21

Week 21

Subject	Thursday	Friday	Comments
Religion	-SSY1: Read p. 71-78		
Spelling	-SF: Administer pre-test. Student writes words in Spelling notebook 3x each that are wrong.	-SF: Take Post-test for grade.	
Grammar	-SJG7WB: p. 96	-SJG7WB: p. 97-98	
Reading	-FW: p. 19-30		
History		-BH: p. 231-236	
Math	-SM7: L. 80	-SMTW7: Test 15	
Science	-SGW7: Read p. 196-214	-SGW7WB: p. 21	
Music Theory			

Subject	Monday	Tuesday	Wednesday
Religion			-LMR7: p. 145-151
Spelling	-SF: p. 117-120, L. 20	-SF: p. 121-122	
Grammar	-SJG7: p. 332-337 (Stop at "Conjunctive Adverbs")	-SJG7WB: p. 99	-SJG7WB: p. 100 (p. 101 extra credit)
Reading	-FW: p. 31-35	-FW: p. 36-42	
History		-BH: p. 237-242	
Math	-SM7: Investigation 8	-SM7: L. 81	-SM7: L. 82 -SMTW7: FPT Q
Science			
Music Theory			-DM1B: p. 24

Week 22

Week 22

Subject	Thursday	Friday	Comments
Religion	-SSYI: Read p. 79-80		
Spelling	-SF: Administer pre-test. Student writes words in Spelling notebook 3x each that are wrong.	-SF: Take Post-test for grade.	
Grammar	-SJG7WB: p. 102	-SJG7WB: p. 103	
Reading	-FW: p. 43-50		
History		-BH: p. 243-248	
Math	-SM7: L. 83	-SM7: L. 84 -SMTW7: FPT R	
Science	-SGW7: Read p. 214-222	-SGW7WB: p. 22	
Music Theory			

Subject	Monday	Tuesday	Wednesday
Religion			-LMR7: p. 151-162
Spelling	SF: p. 123-126, L. 21	-SF: p. 127-128	
Grammar	-SJG7: p. 337-343 (Stop at "The Correct Use of Adverbs")	-SJG7WB: p. 104	-SJG7WB: p. 105
Reading	-FW: p. 51-59	-FW: p. 60-69	
History	-MP: Read p. 1-11	-BH: p. 248-255	
Math	-SM7: L. 85	-SMTW7: Test 16	-SM7: L. 86
Science			
Music Theory			-DMIB: p. 25

Week 23

Week 23

Subject	Thursday	Friday	Comments
Religion			
Spelling	-SF: Administer pre-test. Student writes words in Spelling notebook 3x each that are wrong.	-SF: Take Post-test for grade.	
Grammar	-SJG7WB: p. 106	-SJG7WB: p. 107	
Reading	-FW: p. 70-75		
History		-BH: p. 255-261	
Math	-SM7: L. 87	-SM7: L. 88	
Science	-SGW7: Read p. 222-238	-SGW7WB: p. 23	
Music Theory			

Subject	Monday	Tuesday	Wednesday
Religion			-LMR7: p. 163-169
Spelling	-SF: p. 129-132, L. 22	-SF: p. 133-134	
Grammar	-SJG7: p. 343-347	-SJG7WB: p. 108	-SJG7WB: p. 109
Reading	-FW: p. 76-84	-FW: p. 85-94	
History	-MP: Read p. 12-18	-BH: p. 261-268	
Math	-SM7: L. 89	-SM7: L. 90	-SMTW7: Test 17
Science			
Music Theory			-DMIB: p. 26

Week 24

Week 24			
Subject	Thursday	Friday	Comments
Religion			
Spelling	-SF: Administer pre-test. Student writes words in Spelling notebook 3x each that are wrong.	-SF: Take Post-test for grade.	
Grammar	-SJG7WB: p. 110	-SJG7WB: p. 111 (p. 112 extra credit)	
Reading	-FW: p. 95-106		
History		-BH: p. 268-275	
Math	-SM7: Investigation 9	-SM7: L. 91	
Science	-SGW7: Read p. 243-254	-SGW7WB: p. 24	
Music Theory			

Week 25

Subject	Monday	Tuesday	Wednesday
Religion			-LMR7: p. 169-176
Spelling	-SF: p. 135-138, L. 23	-SF: p. 139-140	
Grammar	-SJG7: p. 348-356 (Stop at "Subordinate Conjunctions")	-SJG7WB: p. 113	-SJG7WB: p. 114
Reading	-FW: p. 107-117	-FW: p. 118-127	
History	-MP: Read p. 19-25	-BH: p. 275-280	
Math	-SM7: L. 92	-SM7: L. 93	-SM7: L. 94 -SMTW7: FPT S
Science			
Music Theory			-DM1B: p. 27

Subject	Thursday	Friday	Comments
Religion			
Spelling	-SF: Administer pre-test. Student writes words in Spelling notebook 3x each that are wrong.	-SF: Take Post-test for grade.	
Grammar	-SJG7WB: p. 115	-SJG7WB: p. 116	
Reading	-FW: p. 128-139		
History		-BH: p. 281-286	
Math	-SM7: L. 95	-SMTW7: Test 18	
Science	-SGW7: Read p. 254-266	-SGW7WB: p. 25	
Music Theory			

Subject	Monday	Tuesday	Wednesday
Religion			-LMR7: p. 176-180
Spelling	-SF: p. 141-144, L. 24	-SF: p. 145-146	
Grammar	-SJG7: p. 356-360	-SJG7WB: p. 117	-SJG7WB: p. 118
Reading	-FW: p. 140-146	-FW: p. 147-154	
History	-MP: Read p. 26-33	-BH: p. 286-292	
Math	-SM7: L. 96	-SM7: L. 97 -SMTW7: FPT T	-SM7: L. 98
Science			
Music Theory			-DM1B: p. 28

Week 26

	Week 26		
Subject	Thursday	Friday	Comments
Religion			
Spelling	-SF: Administer pre-test. Student writes words in Spelling notebook 3x each that are wrong.	-SF: Take Post-test for grade.	
Grammar	-SJG7WB: p. 119	-SJG7WB: p. 120	
Reading	-FW: p. 155-163		
History		-BH: p. 292-298	
Math	-SM7: L. 99	-SM7: L. 100	
Science	-SGW7: p. 266-277 (Teacher may want to mention about how superstitions with the zodiac are sinful and silly)	-SGW7WB: p. 26	
Music Theory			

Week 27

Subject	Monday	Tuesday	Wednesday
Religion			-LMR7: p. 181-191
Spelling			
Grammar	-SJG7: p. 361-369	-SJG7WB: p. 121	-SJG7WB: p. 122 (p. 123 extra credit)
Reading	-FW: p. 164-175	-FW: p. 176-181	
History	-MP: Read p. 34-35	-BH: p. 298-303	
Math	-SMTW7: Test 19	-SM7: Investigation 10 -SMTW7: Activity Sheet 7	-SM7: L. 101
Science			
Music Theory			-DM1B: p. 29

Week 27

Subject	Thursday	Friday	Comments
Religion			
Spelling			
Grammar	-SJG7WB: p. 124 (p. 125 extra credit)	-SJG7WB: p. 126	
Reading	-FW: p. 182-191		
History		-BH: p. 304-309	
Math	-SM7: L. 102	-SM7: L. 103 -SMTW7: FPT U	
Science	-SGW7: Study for Third Quarter Exam (p. 179-278)	-Third Quarter Exam	
Music Theory			

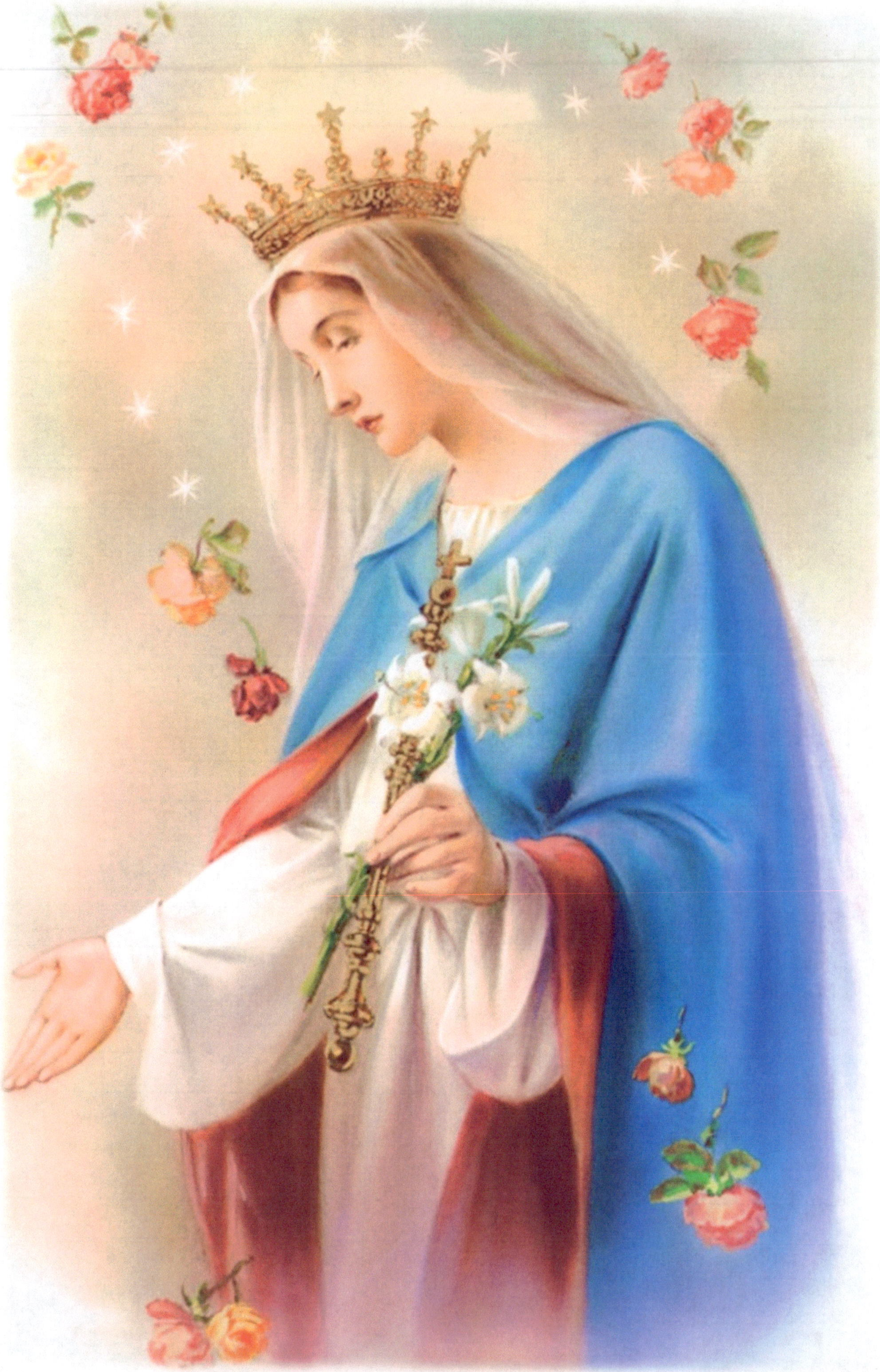

Grade 7
Fourth
Quarter

Week 28

Subject	Monday	Tuesday	Wednesday
Religion			-LMR7: p. 191-198
Spelling	-SF: p. 147-150, L. 25	-SF: p. 151-152	
Grammar	-SJG7: p. 370-373	-SJG7WB: p. 127	-SJG7WB: p. 128
Reading	-FW: p. 192-201	-FW: p. 202-207	-FW: p. 208-216
History	-TCM: Read p. 39-47	-BH: p. 310-315	
Math	-SM7: L. 104	-SM7: L. 105	-SMTW7: Test 20
Science			
Music Theory			-DMIB: p. 30

Week 28

Subject	Thursday	Friday	Comments
Religion			
Spelling	-SF: Administer pre-test. Student writes words in Spelling notebook 3x each that are wrong.	-SF: Take Post-test for grade.	
Grammar	-SJG7WB: p. 129	-SJG7WB: p. 130	
Reading	-FW: p. 217-229		
History		-BH: p. 315-320	
Math	-SM7: L. 106	-SM7: L. 107 -SMTW7: Activity Sheet 8	
Science	-SGW7: Read p. 278-290	-SGW7WB: p. 27	
Music Theory			

Subject	Monday	Tuesday	Wednesday
Religion			-LMR7: p. 198-205
Spelling	-SF: p. 153-156, L. 26	-SF: p. 157-158	
Grammar	-SJG7: p. 374-378 (Stop at "Complex Sentences")	-SJG7WB: p. 131	-SJG7WB: p. 132
Reading	-FW: p. 230-238	-FW: p. 239-244	-FW: p. 245-253
History	-TCM: Read p. 48-52	-BH: p. 321-326	
Math	-SM7: L. 108 -SMTW7: FPT V	-SM7: L. 109	-SM7: L. 110
Science			
Music Theory			-DMIB: p. 31

Week 29

Week 29

Subject	Thursday	Friday	Comments
Religion			
Spelling	-SF: Administer pre-test. Student writes words in Spelling notebook 3x each that are wrong.	-SF: Take Post-test for grade.	
Grammar	-SJG7WB: p. 133	-SJG7WB: p. 134	
Reading	-FW: p. 254-262		
History		-BH: p. 326-332	
Math	-SMTW7: Test 21	-SM7: Investigation 11 -SMTW7: Activity Sheets 9-11	
Science	-SGW7: Read p. 290-299	-SGW7WB: p. 28	
Music Theory			

Week 30

Subject	Monday	Tuesday	Wednesday
Religion			-LMR7: p. 205-214
Spelling	-SF: p. 159-162, L. 27	-SF: p. 163-164	
Grammar	-SJG7: p. 378-384 (Stop at "2. Adverbial Clauses")	-SJG7WB: p. 135	-SJG7WB: p. 136
Reading	-FW: p. 263-269 (end!) Book report	-SJBS: p. 1-8 (about 5 stories a day)	-SJBS: p. 8-15
History	-TCM: Read p. 53-57	-BH: p. 332-339	
Math	-SM7: L. 111	-SM7: L. 112	-SM7: L. 113
Science			
Music Theory			-DM1B: p. 32

Week 30

Subject	Thursday	Friday	Comments
Religion			
Spelling	-SF: Administer pre-test. Student writes words in Spelling notebook 3x each that are wrong.	-SF: Take Post-test for grade.	
Grammar	-SJG7WB: p. 137	-SJG7WB: p. 138	
Reading	-SJBS: p. 15-24		
History		-BH: p. 339-345	
Math	-SM7: L. 114 -SMTW7: FPT W	-SM7: L. 115	
Science	-SGW7: Read p. 299-308	-SGW7WB: p. 29	
Music Theory			

Week 31

Subject	Monday	Tuesday	Wednesday
Religion			-LMR7: p. 215-220
Spelling	SF: p. 165-168, L. 28	-SF: p. 169-170	
Grammar	-SJG7: p. 384-389 (Stop at "Noun Clauses Used as Direct Objects")	-SJG7WB: p. 139	-SJG7WB: p. 140
Reading	-SJBS: p. 24-32	-SJBS: p. 32-40	-SJBS: p. 41-53
History	-TCM: Read p. 58-64 (end!)	-BH: p. 346-351	
Math	-SMTW7: Test 22	-SM7: L. 116	-SM7: L. 117
Science			
Music Theory			-DM1B: p. 33

Week 31

Subject	Thursday	Friday	Comments
Religion			
Spelling	-SF: Administer pre-test. Student writes words in Spelling notebook 3x each that are wrong.	-SF: Take Post-test for grade.	
Grammar	-SJG7WB: p. 141	-SJG7WB: p. 142	
Reading	-SJBS: p. 53-61		
History		-BH: p. 352-356	
Math	-SM7: L. 118	-SM7: L. 119	
Science	-SGW7: Read p. 308-312	-SGW7WB: p. 30	
Music Theory			

Week 32

Subject	Monday	Tuesday	Wednesday
Religion			-LMR7: p. 220-230
Spelling	-SF: p. 171-174, L. 29	-SF: p. 175-176	
Grammar	-SJG7: p. 389-398	-SJG7WB: p. 143	-SJG7WB: p. 144
Reading	-SJBS: p. 61-68	-SJBS: p. 69-80	-SJBS: p. 80-90
History	-Read MGA (the entire book which is quite short)	-BH: p. 357-362	
Math	-SM7: L. 120	-SMTW7: Test 23	-SM7: Investigation 12 -SMTW7: Activity Sheet 12
Science			
Music Theory			-DM1B: p. 34

Week 32

Subject	Thursday	Friday	Comments
Religion			
Spelling	-SF: Administer pre-test. Student writes words in Spelling notebook 3x each that are wrong.	-SF: Take Post-test for grade.	
Grammar	-SJG7WB: p. 145	-SJG7WB: p. 146	
Reading	-SJBS: p. 90-105		
History		-BH: p. 362-368	
Math	-SM7: Topic A, p. 855-857 (end!)		
Science	-SGW7: Read p. 317-325	-SGW7WB: p. 31	
Music Theory			

Week 33

Subject	Monday	Tuesday	Wednesday
Religion			-LMR7: p. 230-235
Spelling	-SF: p. 177-180, L. 30	-SF: p. 181-182	
Grammar	-SJG7: p. 399-406	-SJG7WB: p. 147	-SJG7WB: p. 148
Reading	-SJBS: p. 106-116	-SJBS: p. 116-125	-SJBS: p. 125-130
History	-Remove Map #1 from the back. Give to student to study*	-BH: p. 369-374	
Math			
Science			
Music Theory			-DM1B: p. 35

Week 33

Subject	Thursday	Friday	Comments
Religion			
Spelling	-SF: Administer pre-test. Student writes words in Spelling notebook 3x each that are wrong.	-SF: Take Post-test for grade.	
Grammar	-SJG7WB: p. 149	-SJG7WB: p. 150-151 (p. 152 extra credit)	
Reading	-SJBS: p. 131-138		
History		-BH: p. 375-382	*Show student the list for the test and Map #2 so he knows what to expect on next Monday.
Math			
Science	-SGW7: Read p.325-336	-SGW7WB: p. 32	
Music Theory			

Week 34

Subject	Monday	Tuesday	Wednesday
Religion			-LMR7: p. 235-242
Spelling	-SF: p. 183-186, L. 31	-SF: p. 187-188	
Grammar	-SJG7: p. 407-408	-SJG7WB: p. 153	-SJG7WB: p. 154
Reading	-SJBS: p. 139-150	-SJBS: p. 150-158	-SJBS: p. 158-166
History	-Give test with Map #2 and List. This could be just for fun or grade.	-BH: p. 383-388 (end!)	
Math			
Science			
Music Theory			-DM1B: p. 36

Week 34

Subject	Thursday	Friday	Comments
Religion			
Spelling	-SF: Administer pre-test. Student writes words in Spelling notebook 3x each that are wrong.	-SF: Take Post-test for grade.	
Grammar	-SJG7WB: p. 155	-SJG7WB: p. 156	
Reading	-SJBS: p. 166-176	-SJBS: p. 176-185	
History			
Math			
Science	-SGW7: Read p. 336-352	-SGW7WB: p. 33	
Music Theory			

Week 35

Subject	Monday	Tuesday	Wednesday
Religion			-LMR7: p. 242-248
Spelling	-SF: p. 189-192, L. 32	-SF: p. 193-194	
Grammar	-SJG7: p. 409-413 (Stop at "The Colon")	-SJG7WB: p. 157	-SJG7WB: p. 158
Reading	-SJBS: p. 185-196	-SJBS: p. 197-205	-SJBS: p. 205-213
History	-Remove Map #3 from the back. Give to student to study*		
Math			
Science			
Music Theory			-DM1B: p. 37

Week 35

Subject	Thursday	Friday	Comments
Religion		-LMR7: Student reads p. 250-257 on his own (end!)	
Spelling	-SF: Administer pre-test. Student writes words in Spelling notebook 3x each that are wrong.	-SF: Take Post-test for grade. (end!)	
Grammar	-SJG7WB: p. 159	-SJG7WB: p. 160	
Reading	-SJBS: p. 214-224	-SJBS: p. 224-230	
History			*Show student the list for the test and Map #4 so he knows what to expect on next Monday.
Math			
Science	-SGW7: Read p. 352-365	-SGW7WB: p. 34	
Music Theory			

Subject	Monday	Tuesday	Wednesday
Religion			
Spelling			
Grammar	-SJG7: p. 413-420 (end!)	-SJG7WB: p. 161	-SJG7WB: p. 162
Reading	-SJBS: p. 230-239	-SJBS: p. 239-248	-SJBS: p. 248-254
History		-Give test with Map #4 and List. This could be just for fun or grade.	
Math			
Science			
Music Theory			-DMIB: p. 38

Week 36

Week 36

Subject	Thursday	Friday	Comments
Religion			
Spelling			
Grammar	-SJG7WB: p. 163-164 (end!)		
Reading	-SJBS: p. 254-264 (end!) Book report		
History			
Math			
Science	-SGW7: Study for Third Quarter Exam (p. 278-365)	-Fourth Quarter Exam	
Music Theory		-Eat a bowl of ice cream and maybe give the student one, too! 😉	

LAST DAY OF SCHOOL

St. Jerome School

Grade 7 Report Card for the _____ AD - _____ AD School Year

Student's Name _____

Subject	1st Quarter	2nd Quarter	3rd Quarter	4th Quarter	Final Grade
Religion					
Spelling					
Grammar					
Reading					
History					
Math					
Science					
Music Theory					

PERCENTAGE TO LETTER GRADE CONVERSION

LETTER	A+	A	A-	B+	B	B-	C+
%	97%-100%	93-96%	90%-92%	87%-89%	83%-86%	80%-82%	77%-79%
LETTER	C	C-	D+	D	D-	F	
%	73%-76%	70%-72%	67%-69%	63%-66%	60%-62%	0%-59%	

Notes from Teacher

1st Quarter _____

_____

2nd Quarter _____

_____

3rd Quarter _____

_____

4th Quarter _____

_____

Parent's Signature _____

Antarctica

Map #1

South Atlantic Ocean

South Georgia and the South Sandwich Islands

South Orkney Islands

Falkland Islands

Elephant Island

ARGENTINA

CHILE

Alexander Island

Bellingshausen Sea

Berkner Island

SOUTH POLE

Heard Island and McDonald Islands

Indian Ocean

South Pacific Ocean

0   500   1000 Nautical Miles

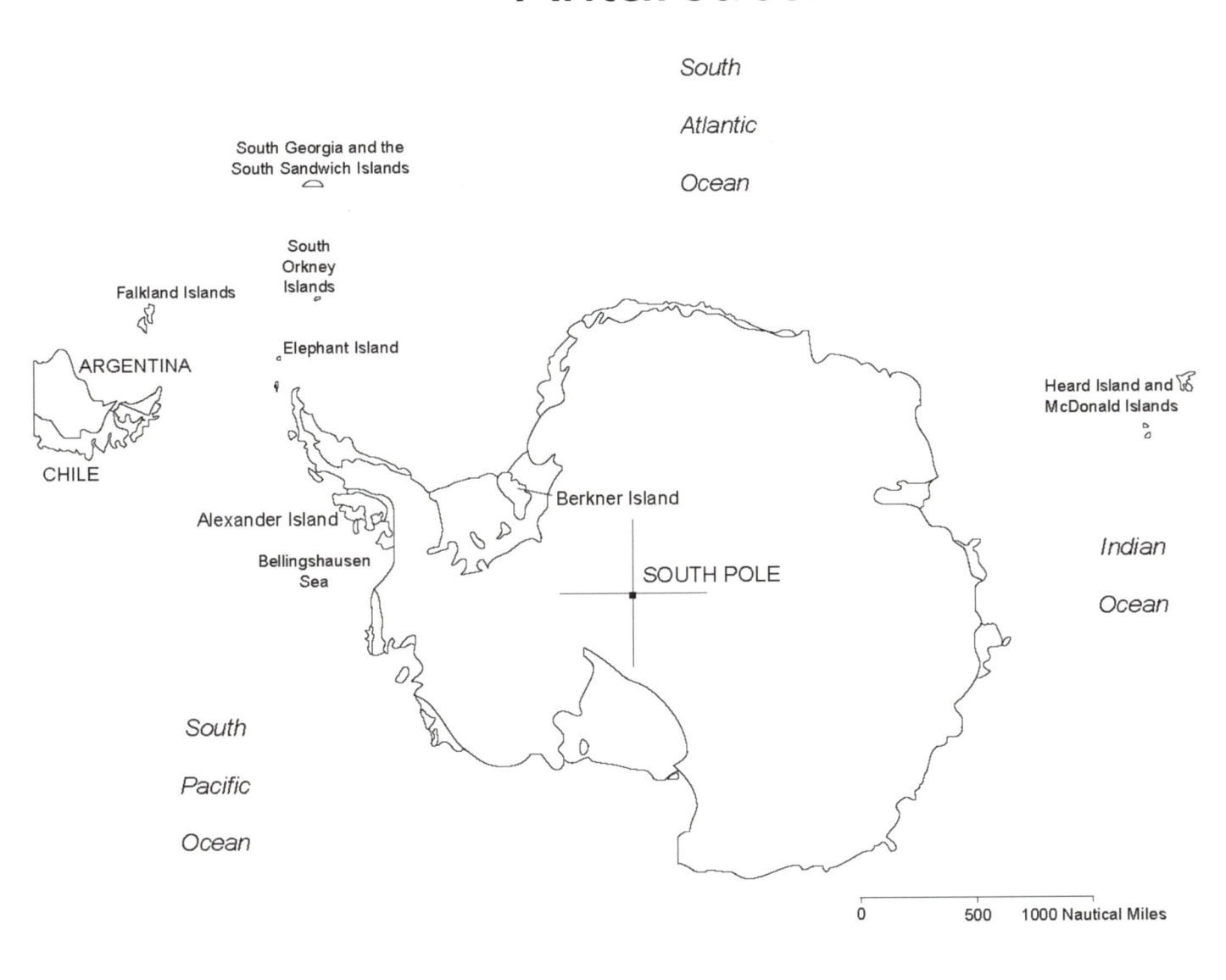

Map #2

Antarctica

Antarctica
List of Countries, Points of Interest, and Bodies of Water for Map #2

Alexander Island
Argentina
Atlantic Ocean
Bellingshausen Sea
Berkner Island
Chile
Elephant Island
Falkland Islands
Heard Island and McDonald Islands
Indian Ocean
Pacific Ocean
South Georgia and the South Sandwich Islands
South Orkney Islands
South Pole

Africa

Map #3

Africa

Map #4

Africa
List of Countries and Bodies of Water for Map #4

Algeria
Angola
Atlantic Ocean
Botswana
Chad
Egypt
Ethiopia
Indian Ocean
Kenya
Libya
Madagascar
Moroco
Mozambique
Niger
Nigeria
Somalia
South Africa
Sudan
Tanzania
Tunisia
Uganda
Zambia
Zimbabwe

SJS Book Report

Book Title:

Author:

Student Name:

Grade:

Submission Date:

Plot (what happened)

Characters

Themes (main idea)

Conflicts and Resolutions

Favorite event

Personal Impressions

Made in the USA
Columbia, SC
06 August 2024